Winter in the Country: Getting Ice, an 1864 lithograph by Currier and Ives, shows a farmer chopping ice from a pond with an ax. The ice was hauled to an ice pit or icehouse for storage and used later.

ICE!

THE AMAZING HISTORY
OF THE ICE BUSINESS

LAURENCE PRINGLE

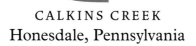

CALKINS CREEK
Honesdale, Pennsylvania

For information about permission to reproduce
selections from this book, please contact
permissions@highlights.com.

Calkins Creek
An Imprint of Boyds Mills Press, Inc.
815 Church Street
Honesdale, Pennsylvania 18431
Printed in China

ISBN: 978-1-59078-801-1

Library of Congress Control Number: 2012937320

First edition

10 9 8 7 6 5 4 3 2 1

Designed by Carla Weise
Production by Margaret Mosomillo
Titles set in Liquorstore
Text set in Plantin

For Sneed B. Collard III,
the last Sneed, and a fine one indeed
—a good writer and a good friend

On a hot summer day, we can be thankful for simple comforts, like running barefoot or swimming in a cool stream or sitting in the shade of a tree. At home, we can be especially thankful for the refrigerator. It stands there, humming quietly to itself. It keeps meat and other foods from spoiling, and chills milk and other drinks. And in its freezer section, ice cream may be waiting, along with ice cubes to make drinks even more refreshing.

It is hard to imagine life without refrigerators and freezers, but they are a "recent" invention. Just a century ago, few homes had such vital appliances. For countless years, people had to find other ways to keep food from spoiling. And for countless generations, most people never had a cold drink on a hot summer day.

For countless generations, most people never had a cold drink on a hot summer day.

This began to change in the early 1800s. Some men in the United States wondered if people could chill food and drink year-round by using a very simple substance: *ice.* Could ice, cut from ponds, lakes, and rivers in the winter, somehow be kept from melting so it could be available in warmer seasons? Could ice be shipped long distances, to southern cities, and even to faraway tropical countries, where ice never occurred naturally? Could selling ice to eager customers in all seasons become an everyday, routine business?

The answers to these questions: *yes, yes,* and *yes!* Harvesting, storing, and transporting ice became a huge business in the United States. Ordinary ice became a necessity for all. In this book, some details of this remarkable "frozen water trade" are told by focusing on one lake that became famous as the "Icebox of New York City."

Customers left ice cards (opposite and page 1) in view for their ice-delivery man. The cards were turned to show, at the top, the pounds of ice needed.

BEFORE REFRIGERATION

Life was very different before refrigeration. Usually, fresh meat, fish, and many other foods had to be eaten in a short span of time. Without cold temperatures, these foods were vulnerable to bacteria that can cause disease. The foods soon began to smell bad and taste bad and became dangerous to eat.

Some steps were taken to keep foods from spoiling (for example, by drying, smoking, and salting). Native Americans air-dried fillets of salmon on wooden racks. Explorers and pioneers sometimes carried jerky—dried, salted strips of meat. Sailing ships stored supplies of salt-cured meat and fish. (Salt draws out the water that bacteria need in order to survive.)

People also tried to keep perishable foods as cool as possible. Temperatures underground are much cooler than aboveground, so farms and homes with gardens often had underground "root cellars," where potatoes, cabbages, carrots, onions, and similar foods were stored. Some landowners dug down as deep as eighteen feet to maintain cool temperatures.

People who lived near spring-fed streams set food containers in water that was chilly year-round. And, throughout history, those who lived in or near high mountains had access to ice. In the Alps of Europe and the high mountain ranges of North and South America, there was year-round snow, glacial ice, and icy-cold streams. (Long ago, ice from the Andes was sold in the city of Lima, Peru.)

Native children in Alaska pose beneath skinned salmon drying in the sun (around 1906).

George Washington's Icehouse Troubles

After leading the Revolutionary army to victory over the British in 1783, George Washington returned to his plantation at Mount Vernon in Virginia. In 1784, he wrote to Robert Morris (U.S. superintendent of finance). Morris had a successful icehouse, and Washington asked for advice because his own icehouse had failed. He wrote that the ice was "gone already" by early June. Morris replied with detailed plans—walls, roof, floor, insulation, and especially a way to allow water from the melted ice to drain away. Washington continued to report to Robert Morris about his efforts in building better icehouses at his home in Mount Vernon—even after he became the first president of the United States, in 1789.

Visitors at Monticello can look down into Thomas Jefferson's rock-walled icehouse, built in 1802, where ice was stored.

Ice was also a luxury available to those with great power or wealth. Historians report that both Alexander the Great and Roman emperor Nero Claudius Caesar ordered their slaves to bring ice from high in the mountains so they could have refreshing drinks. (Caesar was fond of fruit drinks.) Slaves also helped provide ice at Monticello, the Virginia plantation of Thomas Jefferson, the third president of the United States. Monticello had a thick-walled underground space that could hold sixty-two wagonloads of ice, brought up from the Rivanna River.

Elsewhere, in colder parts of North America, some landowners had belowground ice pits or aboveground icehouses. Groups of farmers or townspeople sometimes worked together to harvest ice and share it. They tried to make the ice last as long as possible, using different materials as insulation: hay, wood shavings, and sawdust (tiny bits of wood that fall as saw blades cut through wood).

Despite such efforts, the last ice had usually melted by August or September.

This meant no more ice for at least three or four months! Still, having *any* ice last far into the summer was a treat denied to most people of those times.

USA
34

ROBERT FAWCETT

2001

The cold, hard work of ice harvesting is shown in a painting by Robert Fawcett, reproduced in a 2001 U.S. postage stamp.

ICE FOR EVERYONE!

Some men dreamed of making ice available year-round. One had even more ambitious dreams. Frederic Tudor came from a wealthy Boston family. The family estate, Rockwood, included a pond from which ice was cut and stored and later used to make ice cream and to chill drinks in summertime. This childhood experience gave Frederic Tudor a business idea when he was nearly twenty-two years old. In August 1805, Tudor wrote of his plan "for transporting Ice to Tropical Climates." Frederic was joined by his older brother, William, but he was the driving force of the business. Although he wrote in his journal that "People only laugh and believe me not when I tell them I am going to carry ice to the West Indies," he dedicated his life to achieving his goal. In the process, he inspired others to make discoveries and inventions for cutting, storing, and transporting ice. In the 1800s, he was called the "Ice King," and today Frederic Tudor is called the "father of the ice industry."

Tudor's dream of selling ice soon led to important changes in ice harvesting. The common practice was to use axes to chop ice from lakes, ponds, and rivers. The irregular pieces were loaded into carts and wagons and taken to be stored. Because of their odd shapes, the ice melted rather quickly. (Irregular pieces expose more surface area to the air than do pieces with smooth, flat surfaces. The greater the exposure to air, the faster the ice melts.) Men also cut ice with saws.

Frederic Tudor's ice-exporting business lost money for fourteen years. Tudor kept trying, for he believed that a man who gives up "has never been, is not, and never will be, a hero in war, love or business."

Nathaniel Wyeth's invention of horse-drawn ice cutters (called ice plows) helped the ice business grow. The plows quickly cut into ice in straight lines (here, near Sandusky, Ohio).

This produced blocks of ice with more even sides, but the work was slow and difficult. Then in 1827, Nathaniel J. Wyeth invented a horse-drawn ice cutter. With this saw, ice could be cut quickly into squares and rectangles. This made the ice easier to transport and store, and the ice blocks melted more slowly than irregular pieces.

Frederic Tudor and others also tried to find better ways to store ice. Some melting was inevitable; the challenge was to keep it to a minimum. One surprising discovery: storing ice aboveground, in an icehouse, was often better than storing it belowground. Underground, the bottommost ice might sit in meltwater, which caused more thawing. In a well-built icehouse, the floor was off the ground, not resting on it. This allowed meltwater to drain away. Since dark colors absorb solar energy, the walls and sometimes even the roofs of icehouses were painted white to reflect sunlight. Finally, a well-built icehouse was windowless, had its entrance door facing north, and had vents in its roof to allow any heat to escape.

Ice-Tool Inventor

Nathaniel Jarvis Wyeth led ice harvesting at Fresh Pond, a lake near Boston. In 1826, Frederic Tudor hired Wyeth to take charge of cutting, storing, and loading all ice supplies for his growing business. Tudor wrote that Wyeth was "just enough of a schemer and inventor to be valuable." How true: Wyeth invented many ice-cutting tools and devices for lifting heavy ice blocks. When he died in 1856, a Boston newspaper wrote, "There is not a single tool or machine of real value now employed in the ice harvesting, which was not originally invented by Mr. Wyeth."

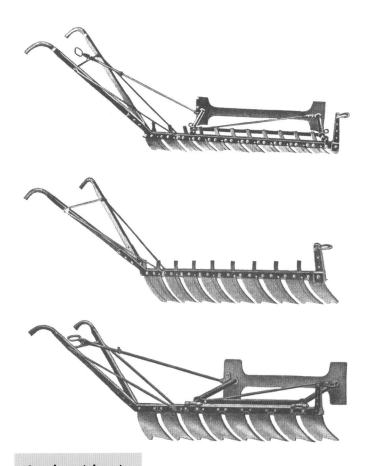

Ice plows (above) varied in their number of steel cutting teeth and the depths they cut. Right: A boy loads ice into an icebox after hanging his ice tongs on the door.

Whether ice was stored, or transported by wagons, ships, or trains, it had to be insulated to prevent melting. Many kinds of insulation were tried, including hay, straw, and charcoal. In 1806, hay was used as insulation for ice loaded on a sailing ship bound from Boston to Martinique in the Caribbean Sea. Much of the ice melted on the long voyage. (At first, Frederic Tudor had trouble hiring sailors because they feared that the ice cargo would melt quickly, fill the ship with water, and cause it to sink! Then, because ice was such a novelty in Martinique, Tudor had trouble selling the remaining ice. It was 1820 before his long-distance ice business became profitable.) Eventually, people learned that dry sawdust—spread between and around blocks of ice—was the best insulation. (Wet sawdust could be dried, then reused.) At lumber mills, sawdust had been worthless waste. Thanks to the growing ice business, it became a valuable commodity.

Another challenge for pioneers and inventors of the ice business was making an insulated container for storing ice in homes, restaurants, saloons, and hotels. In 1803, a Maryland farmer and engineer named Thomas Moore described such a device in a pamphlet entitled *An Essay on the Most Eligible Construction of Ice-Houses: Also a Description of the Newly Invented Machine Called the Refrigerator.* That term—*refrigerator*—was used long before the invention of the electric-powered appliance we know today. Still, most people called the first kind of refrigerator an "icebox." It was made of wood, with an inner lining of iron or porcelain and with insulation material between the wood and the lining. Like an icehouse, an icebox needed to get rid of

An advertisement from 1890

Why Is It Called *Ice* Cream?

There is no ice in ice cream, yet ice has played a crucial role in making ice cream. Once ice became widely available in the United States, restaurants and street vendors sold this popular frozen treat. Some families had a tradition of making it on Sunday.

An old-fashioned ice-cream maker consisted of a metal can set inside a small wooden barrel. To make ice cream, first the ingredients were mixed. They included cream, sugar, and eggs, plus other ingredients, depending on the desired flavor (for example, fruit or chocolate). This mixture was poured into the metal can, which was then sealed with a metal lid.

Next, ice chips and rock salt were put into the barrel, surrounding and covering the sealed can. Within the can was a *dasher* (a kind of beater), which was connected to a handle. This allowed someone to keep stirring the cream and other ingredients.

Mixing salt and ice created a brine with a temperature below freezing. This drew heat out of the metal can, gradually freezing the ingredients inside. Steady stirring kept the ice cream from freezing solid. Sometimes more ice and salt were added to the brine to ensure cold-enough temperatures. The ice cream was usually ready after about twenty minutes of steady cranking. Children often had the chore of turning the handle that moved the dasher—a job with a delicious payoff.

meltwater (via a tube leading to a pan beneath). Through the years, icebox designs improved, and they became better insulated. (Thomas Moore had tried insulation of rabbit fur. Fortunately for rabbits, their fur was a poor ice insulator.)

Iceboxes became common in homes, restaurants, and hotels. Thanks to the persistence of Frederic Tudor, Nathaniel Wyeth, and many others, the ice business grew and grew. In major U.S. cities, ice was no longer a luxury for the wealthy. It was affordable for nearly everyone. During the early 1800s, visitors from England and Europe—where the ice business developed

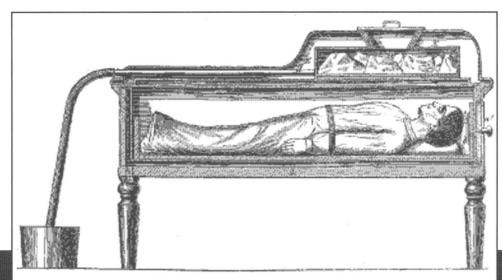

BUNN'S CORPSE PRESERVER.

Icebox for the Dead

The December 6, 1862, issue of *Scientific American* described the patent for an improved product that used ice: Bunn's Corpse Preserver. It resembled a long, horizontal icebox, with an upper compartment that held ice above the head and upper body of the corpse within. Ice chilled the air in the entire enclosed space. This was an improvement on earlier methods that used ice to preserve dead bodies until they were buried.

These old postcards show ice cutting on Lake Erie (top) and on Chautauqua Lake in western New York (center) and an ice delivery wagon in Cedar Rapids, Iowa (bottom).

slowly—were amazed at the abundance of iced drinks, ice cream, and other frozen treats in America.

By 1847, Frederic Tudor's ice-exporting business was thriving. Sailing ships from Boston carried ice to southern ports—Norfolk, Charleston, Savannah, New Orleans. Cargoes of ice also reached Cuba, Brazil, and India. (Four or five months were needed for a ship to travel sixteen thousand miles to India. Even though about half of the ice aboard melted, this was a commercial success.)

In the late 1800s, more than twenty-five million tons of ice were sold annually in the United States. Frederic Tudor's ice company in Boston continued to lead in shipping ice to the South, the Caribbean, and distant nations. Meanwhile, ice had become a vital product in other U.S. cities. In the 1850s, ice from Alaska was shipped to San Francisco. In Chicago, the ice business started in 1847, with ice taken from the north branch of the Chicago River. At first, just one wagon was needed to deliver ice to customers in that small city (population: 28,000). By the 1860s, Chicago needed ice from several dozen huge icehouses that stored ice from lakes in Illinois, Indiana, and Wisconsin. The city had become the livestock-slaughtering center of the country. Chicago butchers and meat-packing companies needed ice for storing meat and to chill railroad cars that carried their products to markets.

Ice Advice for Housewives, 1868

"Ice has two 'natural enemies,' warm air and water, but the latter is by far the more deadly. Water at 40 degrees will melt ice with 10 times the rapidity of air at 80 degrees."

—*Godey's Lady's Book and Magazine*, July 1868

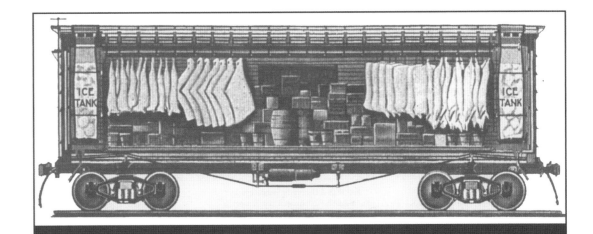

Cool Cars

The invention of an ice-cooled railroad car was patented in 1867. It was well insulated and had floor-to-ceiling ice-storage spaces at each end. Its design allowed chilled air to circulate through the cargo, which could include not only meat but also seafood, dairy products, fruit, and other foods that required refrigeration during days of travel.

As ice became vital across America, the ice business had far-reaching effects. It offered work in the winter to countless thousands of men who harvested and stored ice, to many others who operated barges and ships to transport it, and to still others who delivered ice to customers all year long. Many who had no direct contact with ice also benefited. They included mechanics, blacksmiths, carpenters, and workers in grocery and clothing stores that served the families of the ice workers.

ICE FOR NEW YORK CITY

In 1800, the population of New York City was about 79,000. Forests grew and land was farmed in an area that is now packed with several million people and many tall buildings. City residents harvested ice from ponds and from the Bronx River. Eventually, these nearby sources became polluted by human and animal wastes. The growing city had to reach out for ever-increasing amounts of good-quality ice.

Thirty miles north, and conveniently just a half mile west of the Hudson River, lay a 279-acre lake. Native Americans had called it Quaspeake, meaning "spearing place" in Algonquian. (They fished its clear waters, sometimes using spears.) European settlers called it simply "the pond" until 1835, when it was named Rockland Lake. It is in New York State's Rockland County, where rock was, and still is, quarried for use in construction.

The lake is enclosed by hills, including a long rocky ridge called Hook Mountain that separates it from the Hudson. However, near the lake's northeast end is a "clove"—a low gap in the ridge, providing an easy route to the river. (*Clove* comes from the Dutch word *kloof*, which means "cleft," "gap," or "ravine.") The lake's handy access to the river helped in transporting ice by ship or barge to New York City. More important, however, was the lake's high-quality water. Though small streams flow into Rockland Lake, most of its water arises from springs beneath its surface. For city people worried about pollution, pure ice from Rockland Lake was a treasure.

For city people worried about pollution, pure ice from Rockland Lake was a treasure.

Rockland Lake nestles in a valley beyond the rocky ridge called Hook Mountain.
The Hudson River flows by on the right side and bottom of this old postcard photo.

Knickerbocker Engine Company No. 1 was founded in 1862, after fire destroyed a huge icehouse at Rockland Lake.

In 1830, three men prepared to sell ice from Rockland Lake by first digging an ice-storage pit twenty feet square and fifteen feet deep. Lined with straw for insulation, it held about 125 tons of ice that was cut from the lake in early 1831. Even though some had melted by summer, the remaining ice was carried by steamboat to New York City for sale. By 1833, the men had formed a company (Barmore, Felter, and Company) and built a 1,500-ton-capacity icehouse by Rockland Lake.

Demand for the lake's ice led to competition, with three companies cutting ice. By 1855, the companies joined, forming the Knickerbocker Ice Company. It was created "for collecting, storing, and preserving ice, of preparing it for sale, of transporting it to the City of New York or elsewhere, and of vending the same."

"Elsewhere" indeed! In 1860, a local newspaper, the *Rockland County Journal*, reported that the company had "increased the shipment of ice to India, Australia,

Knickerbocker

Knickerbocker is a Dutch word that means "marble baker." It was a common last name in the area now called New York City, in a region colonized by the Dutch. (Until 1664, the city's name was New Amsterdam.) Anyone who lived in or near the city might be called a "Knickerbocker." In the 1840s, the name was given to one of the nation's first baseball teams, and the Knickerbocker Rules were among the first basic rules of the game. Today, Knickerbocker Avenue in Brooklyn and the professional basketball team New York Knickerbockers—the Knicks—remind us of New York's Dutch origins.

Drawings in an 1869 issue of *American Agriculturist* show some of the steps in an ice harvest, this one at Rockland Lake. Figure 5 (bottom left) shows inclined elevators, powered by a steam engine. Built in 1860, they carried blocks of ice up and into an icehouse, where workers stored them in layers.

The Ice Harvest.

But few are aware of the importance of the ice harvest. It has been derisively said of Massachusetts that her principal productions were granite and ice. The first shipments of ice to India and other tropical countries, were made from Boston, and the ice trade has had much to do, directly and indirectly, with the prosperity of that city. The ice trade is by no means an important one to Boston only, but in New York and near every considerable town and city there are large amounts invested in the ice business, and employment given to thousands of laborers. The immense demand of New York City for ice, is met by several associations, the largest of which is the Knickerbocker Ice Co., which draws its supplies from Rockland Lake. This lake is about half a mile west of the Hudson River, and a short distance above the town of Nyack; its water is remarkably pure and clear, and it is so situated as to afford unusual facilities for gathering and shipping the ice. One of our artists visited this locality during the harvest of last year, and presents a series of sketches which show the different steps in securing the crop. The ice is first cleared, if necessary, of fallen snow, as shown in figure 1. V-shaped snow-plows and common road-scrapers are used. Figure 2 shows the process of marking and cutting. The cleared surface is marked by an iron point, as a guide for the ice-plow, which is a blade with coarse teeth, like a series of plane-irons placed one after another. This when drawn across the ice makes a deep groove or furrow. Attached to one side of the plow is a guide which runs in one groove, and serves to mark the distance of the next one. When the ice is sufficiently grooved by the plow, it may be split up by the use of an iron bar terminated below by a heavy chisel. A saw with coarse teeth is also used for dividing the ice; it has a cross-handle, and is worked by one man. Figure 3 shows the operations of sawing and "barring off" large masses, which have already been marked by the plow. These are floated towards the ice-house by the aid of horses, as represented in figure 4. The houses,

Fig. 1.—CLEARING THE ICE OF SNOW.

Fig. 2.—MARKING AND CUTTING.

Fig. 3.—SAWING AND BARRING OFF.

Fig. 4.—CANALING TO THE HOUSE.

Fig. 5.—THE ELEVATORS.

Fig. 6.—PACKING AWAY THE ICE.

and other foreign ports over three hundred percent. Within the last half dozen years it has grown up to be an immense business, embracing within its folds nearly every known land."

The high quality of Rockland Lake ice became known worldwide. When the luxurious Astor House hotel opened in New York City in 1836, it advertised to potential guests that it used ice from Rockland Lake. In Norway (the only nation besides the United States to export ice), an ice company renamed one of its lakes "Rockland Lake" to help its ice sales in London!

At the original Rockland Lake, for many years ice had been lifted into the icehouses by horsepower. Horses pulled on ropes, hauling wooden containers of ice up elevators. This was a slow process. After each load, both the horse and the elevator had to return to their starting point. The year 1860 brought a great improvement: steam-powered elevators that could run continuously, carrying ice up inclined planes into different levels of the icehouses.

People treasured high-quality ice from Rockland Lake. Although the lake could not supply all the ice needed for New York City's growing population, ice from other sources was still advertised as "Rockland Lake ice."

In this 1852 engraving, Hook Mountain looms above the Barmore icehouse by Rockland Lake. The artist added a huge flag that probably did not exist, but the artist accurately drew vertical ice elevators, powered by horses, in front of the building. This huge icehouse burned down in 1861.

By 1860, three huge white icehouses gleamed by the lake's northeast end. They had foundations of 4-foot-thick stone walls and stood 40 feet tall. Their floor plans measured longer than a football field. (Counting end zones, football fields are 360 feet in length.)

Biggest of all was the Barmore icehouse: 550 feet long and 100 feet wide. Inside, ice was stored in thirteen separate rooms. To help reduce melting, all big icehouses were divided into several rooms. Walls separating the rooms were filled with sawdust insulation. Unfortunately, fire was always a threat to icehouses. They were kept as dry as possible, and both sawdust and wooden walls burn readily. In the winter of 1861, when the mighty Barmore icehouse was three-quarters full of ice, it was destroyed by fire. That spring, a volunteer fire company was formed: the Knickerbocker Fire Engine No. 1 of Rockland Lake. It still exists.

WORKING ON THE ICE

Most ice harvesting was done in January and February, when lakes, ponds, and rivers were usually deeply frozen. Ice had to be at least five inches thick to support the weight of horses and men. (Ice ten inches thick was ideal for producing blocks that would eventually fit in iceboxes.) The season brought no shortage of workers. Winter was an idle time for farmers as well as laborers with jobs such as rock quarrying and brickmaking. North of Rockland Lake lay the town of Haverstraw. Deposits of clay there made Haverstraw a major brickmaking center. Winter weather halted most of that work, so many brickmakers were eager to earn some money. (Idle workers from the brick industry near Boston also provided much of the labor for ice harvesting in that area.)

At Rockland Lake, under ideal conditions, as many as six hundred men were hired for three or four weeks to fill the icehouses. Wages were a

For a Dollar a Day

From his home in New York's Catskill Mountains, naturalist and essayist John Burroughs could watch an ice harvest in progress: "Sometimes nearly two hundred men and boys with numerous horses, are at work at once, marking, ploughing, planing, scraping, sawing, hauling, chiseling . . . while knots and straggling lines of idlers here and there look on in cold discontent, unable to get a job." Burroughs knew the importance of this work for many: "Ice or no ice," he wrote, "sometimes means bread or no bread to scores of families."

Workers and horses gather to cut ice at Rockland Lake in the late 1880s.

dollar a day (two dollars for a skilled mechanic). Timing was crucial for a good harvest of ice. A sudden thaw that softened the ice surface could bring work to a halt. When conditions were right, work often began at four or five a.m., and sometimes continued into the night, with lanterns providing light for the workers. A snowstorm did not halt the harvest, but it made the job more difficult and expensive: Snow had to be cleared from the cutting area to reach the ice. And snow removal increased the cost of labor. Snow clearing was needed for another reason, too. Snow is an insulator. When the snow was removed, cold air was able to freeze the water more deeply.

Men guided horses pulling saws to cut a checkerboard pattern of grooves in the ice surface. Then another kind of horse-drawn saw was used to cut much deeper into the ice. Men broke off blocks by striking into the deep grooves with long-handled chisels (also called breaking bars). A narrow canal of open water was cut—and kept from freezing—so that horses, or men with long spiked poles, could pull or push ice blocks along this channel to the shore, near an icehouse. Before storage, big blocks of ice were usually cut into smaller pieces for easier handling.

In the icehouse, once workers had set down a layer of ice blocks, the men spread sawdust on top, then started a new layer. Block by block,

Girl on the Ice!

The ice business was considered the work of men, including teenage boys (many of whom ended their schooling before high school), who were eager to earn a wage. Women were excluded, as they were from many other jobs in the early 1900s. At Rockland Lake, however, there was one exception: Josephine Walter. She was born and raised in the area. She and her family knew many men who worked "on the ice." In the winter of 1917, seventeen-year-old Josephine was hired to guide horses as they hauled blocks of ice to the giant ice-storage buildings.

"I would lead the horse out onto the lake, hook up the ice with a chain and the horse would pull it through the canals to the ice houses. It wasn't dangerous if you watched where you walked, although horses did fall through sometimes.

"I was the only girl to work on the ice and a lot of the fellows didn't like working with a girl," she recalled. Her employment that winter was kept secret. At Rockland Lake, "They put my name down as Joe so the Knickerbocker Ice Company wouldn't know."

Josephine later married a mechanic, George Hudson. With him she raised three children in a house that still overlooks the lake where she was the first, and last, female to work "on the ice." Josephine lived for eighty-six years and died in 1985.

Josephine Walter guided horses that pulled big slabs of ice to the icehouses.

Horses, Lots of Horses

Countless thousands of horses played key roles in every step of the process of harvesting ice and in moving ice from lake surface to city customer. The ice business also needed people to feed and care for them. At Rockland Lake, a large barn provided shelter for as many as sixty horses. Those that worked directly on the ice usually had special studded or spiked shoes to help prevent slipping and falling. One worker—typically a teenage boy—had an unpleasant job: cleaning horse droppings and urine from the ice. He pulled a small sled or sleigh with a waterproof lining. Droppings were scooped up with a shovel, and ice was scraped away to remove urine. Sometimes formaldehyde was poured on the ice to kill germs.

In cities, blocks of ice were loaded onto horse-drawn wagons for delivery to customers. Thousands of horses needed food, water, shelter, and the work of blacksmiths who maintained iron horseshoes.

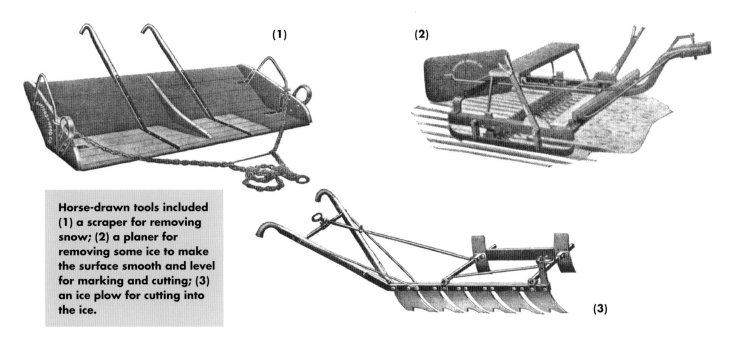

Horse-drawn tools included (1) a scraper for removing snow; (2) a planer for removing some ice to make the surface smooth and level for marking and cutting; (3) an ice plow for cutting into the ice.

row by row, layer by layer, room by room, huge amounts of ice were stored in an icehouse—as much as one hundred thousand tons.

Ice harvest time was concentrated in a few weeks of deep winter. It attracted crowds of onlookers, drawn to the spectacle of hundreds of men and dozens of horses working all day, and sometimes at night, on the precious "silver harvest."

Within an icehouse, men worked fast to store blocks of ice into rows and layers.

ICE TOOLS

A 1919 catalog offered all sorts of equipment for the ice business. It included a variety of heavy steel breaking bars and chisels (right-hand page) used to harvest and handle ice.

NO. 630
SPLITTING AWL. ROUND HANDLE

NO. 628.   ADVERTISING AWLS

NO. 642
HAND SAW, OVAL IRON HANDLE, 30 IN.

Weight, 4½ lbs.; blade, 30 in. long.

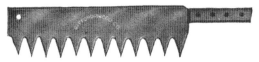

NO. 648.   ICE CLEAVER OR HACK

Weight, 3 lbs.; length of blade, 20 in.

NO. 700
IRONCLAD

Weight, 5¼ lbs.

NO. 707
MOGUL

Weight, 6¼ lbs.

NO. 635
CHIPPER. WOOD HANDLE

4¾-in. x 2¾-in. blade.

NO. 636
CHIPPER, IRON HANDLE

4¾-in. x 2¾-in. blade.

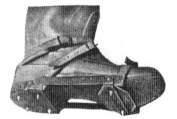

NO. 679A
G-W ICE CREEPER. STYLE A

NO. 679B
G-W ICE CREEPER. STYLE B

NO. 443.   SPLITTING FORK, RING HANDLE, WEIGHT 18 LBS.

NO. 457.   CALKING BAR, HOLLOW HANDLE, WEIGHT 8 LBS.

NO. 458.   BAR CHISEL, STEEL HANDLE, WEIGHT 15½ LBS.

NO. 460.   SUMMER BAR, CURVED BLADE, HEAVY WEIGHT, 17 LBS.

NO. 465.   STARTING CHISEL, WEIGHT 14½ LBS.

NO. 477.   SPLITTING CHISEL, RING HANDLE, WEIGHT 14 LBS.

NO. 480.   SAW TOOTH CHISEL, RING HANDLE, WEIGHT 14 LBS.

NO. 484.   CANAL NEEDLE BAR, RING HANDLE, WEIGHT 11 LBS.

NO. 486.   NEEDLE BAR, 3 TINED, RING HANDLE, WEIGHT 16½ LBS.

NO. 495.   SEPARATING CHISEL, KNOB HANDLE, WEIGHT 14 LBS.

NO. 502.   ELEVATOR FORK, WEIGHT 3¾ LBS.

An old postcard shows a thriving Rockland Lake community, with an icehouse (right) and the clove (left) through which ice was brought to the Hudson River.

GETTING ICE TO THE RIVER

The biggest challenge to delivering ice from Rockland Lake to New York City was getting it to the edge of the Hudson River. At first, horses hauled loads of ice uphill through the clove. The ice was then lowered through a chute down the steep hillside to the river. (Ice blocks had to be lowered slowly. Workers found that out when an unbraked block of ice hurtled downhill with such speed that it passed right through a riverside icehouse and splashed into the river beyond!) A better system was needed. The Knickerbocker Ice Company hired engineers to plan and build one: an inclined railroad. It was finished, and celebrated with a champagne reception, on September 25, 1860. This exciting development attracted visitors from up and down the Hudson.

The railroad had a number of small cars that moved on parallel tracks, but it had no locomotive. Horses pulled the cars, loaded with ice, along several hundred feet of tracks. Then, at the bottom of the hill, each car was

The inclined railroad carried loads of ice through the clove, down to docks at the river's edge.

31

Icehouses, as long as football fields, could store many thousands of tons of ice.

Each block of ice weighed two hundred to three hundred pounds. In one hour, a steam-powered elevator could lift as many as 175 tons of ice up and into an icehouse.

pulled uphill along tracks by a strong chain, powered from a steam-engine house. Horses helped again at the top of the clove, pulling the railroad cars across the level area to the brow of the slope that led down to the river. Gravity brought the ice-filled cars downhill. Brakes, and the weight of empty railroad cars being pulled uphill, slowed the descent. Near the river, horses sometimes pulled the ice-laden cars along a thousand feet of track and onto the dock, where barges waited for their loads. (If ice could not be transported right away, it was stored in a riverside icehouse.)

The ice business thrived, and so did the community that grew near the lake. A post office opened in 1842. Homes, churches, stores, and a school were built. In the early 1880s, railroad tracks

Ice from Walden Pond

In the winter of 1846–1847, Boston's need for ice reached Walden Pond, about fifteen miles northwest of the city. The sixty-one-acre pond later became famous through the writings of philosopher Henry David Thoreau, who wrote *Walden; or, Life in the Woods*. In the late 1840s, however, the pond was simply another source of ice for Frederic Tudor's ice business. Thoreau lived in a log cabin by the shore of Walden Pond and witnessed the process of cutting and storing the ice. He enjoyed talking to and joking with small numbers of local ice harvesters but was annoyed when a hundred men came to cut ice to ship far away. Still, he marveled at the possibility of the ice being shipped to Madras, Bombay, or Calcutta, in India, where perhaps "The pure Walden water is mingled with the sacred water of the Ganges."

reached the lake, and trains began carrying some of the lake's high-quality ice to faraway markets. On summer weekends and holidays, special trains brought visitors to a lakeside picnic area.

Meanwhile, the Knickerbocker Ice Company's steamboats pushed ice-laden barges from the Hudson's shore near Rockland Lake downriver to New York City.

Barges cluster by docks at the edge of the Hudson River, ready to load with ice.

ICE HOUSES ON THE HUDSON.

DOWN THE RIVER TO NEW YORK.

DISTRIBUTING TO THE WAGONS.

SUPPLYING AN OCEAN STEAMER.

WEIGHING A LOAD.

SMALL CUSTOMERS.

An 1884 engraving, *The Ice Industry of New York*, shows an upriver icehouse, ice-laden barges on the Hudson River, ice being loaded onto an ocean steamer, and Knickerbocker Ice Company wagons delivering ice all through New York City.

HERE COMES THE ICEMAN!

Dawn in nineteenth-century New York City brought the rumbles and rattles of many horse-drawn delivery wagons. Some hauled ice from the edge of the Hudson or East Rivers, where blocks of ice were unloaded from barges. Although the city had icehouses, most of the ice was taken directly from the barges.

Barges brought ice from Rockland Lake but also from other sources. Even though Rockland Lake was once called the "Icebox of New York City," it was probably never the city's sole ice supply. Of course, thanks to the lake's reputation for high-quality ice, some delivery wagons were proudly marked "Ice from Rockland Lake." However, with each passing year, this advertisement became less accurate. The lake's harvest could not keep up with the city's growing demand.

In 1866, eighty thousand tons of ice were taken from Rockland Lake, but that amount supplied only about 20 percent of the city's growing needs. Both the Knickerbocker Ice Company and its rival, the New York Ice Company, reached farther and farther from the city for ice. The Hudson River north of Poughkeepsie was a major source. (The river is an estuary and usually contains some salty ocean water south of Poughkeepsie.) Other ice sources included the Mohawk River, which flows into the Hudson, and lakes in upstate New York, northern New Jersey, and Pennsylvania.

As the demand for ice grew, scores of giant icehouses lined the shores of the Hudson River, and many thousands of laborers brought in the winter harvest.

In 1877, the Knickerbocker Ice Company owned 600 delivery wagons and about 1,000 horses. Its main competitor used 180 wagons and 300 horses. Icemen and their horses had a tough job. They usually rested on Sunday, but on other days they traveled from ten to fifteen miles in the city and even farther on suburban routes. Before and after working a ten-hour day, an iceman had to feed and care for his horse.

The wagons carried blocks of ice that measured 22 inches by 30 inches, or 22 inches by 28 inches, and were never less than 10 inches thick. Cut in half to fit many iceboxes, each weighed about 60 pounds. Each day, an iceman delivered several hundred of these blocks to apartments and other homes, lifting and carrying them with tongs or hoisting them onto one shoulder or in a strong canvas bag. He often carried ice blocks up several flights of stairs. The iceman followed regular routes and customers. Often the

A Horse Named Jerry, or "White Silver"

On March 4, 1908, while a Brooklyn iceman named Adolph Metzer quickly ate lunch, he left his wagon, loaded with 1,800 pounds of ice, and his workhorse, Jerry. When he returned, all were gone. Metzer gave the police a detailed description of the stolen wagon and his horse. Jerry was all white except for a distinctive black scar on his right flank. Months passed. Jerry and the wagon were still missing. Then, in July, a Brooklyn detective stopped to watch an open-air circus in Luna Park in Brooklyn's Coney Island. One attraction was "White Silver," a handsome white horse that leaped through colored hoops. The detective remembered the missing Jerry, examined the horse, and found a black scar on its right flank, partly hidden by white powder.

The circus owner revealed the seller's name, and an arrest was made. Alas, newspapers failed to report what happened next. Most likely, the circus career of White Silver ended, and Jerry returned to the unglamorous job of hauling an ice wagon.

Many Sources of Ice

Figures from the 1866 ice harvest, as reported by New York City's two biggest ice companies, revealed that most ice was cut near towns far up the Hudson River.

NEW YORK ICE COMPANY		KNICKERBOCKER ICE COMPANY	
Towns	**Tons of Ice**	**Towns**	**Tons of Ice**
Athens	55,000	Clearwater	17,000
Catskill	50,000	Coxsackie	30,000
Evesport	13,000	Esopus	30,000
Marlboro	18,000	Kingston Creek	5,000
New Baltimore	10,000	New Paltz	16,000
Poughkeepsie	25,000	Rhinebeck	25,000
Stratsburg	25,000	Rockland Lake	80,000
		Turkey Point	10,000

horse pulling the wagon knew the route as well as the iceman did. While the man delivered ice to one customer, the horse pulled the ice wagon ahead and stopped in front of the next customer's home! Customers left cardboard signs that indicated the amount of ice needed—usually 25, 50, 75, or 100 pounds.

Telephone Lebanon 578

Air Conditioned ICE Refrigeration

HANOVER ICE COMPANY

Put this card in the Window where we can see it.

Ice cards served as advertisements and as a way to tell icemen how much ice to deliver. Some cards had a dial, turned to the number of pounds needed. Most cards were simply placed in a window with the desired number at the top. A variety of colorful ice cards is shown on the following four pages.

AMERICAN ICE CARDS

NO ICE

15   20

SPRING BROOK

ICE

50   25

Phone 4374   SERVICE   H. E. DOERR, Prop.

40   35   30

40
POUNDS

60
POUNDS

Natural and
Manufactured Ice

FUEL, FURNACE AND
RANGE OIL

MASSASOIT LAKE ICE CO.
E. J. NOONAN, Prop.

Office : 212 Eastern Ave.

Telephone 7-4311

POUNDS

80

15
CENTS

See the New Air-Conditioned Refrigerators

25

100   **50**

FOODS WON'T DRY OUT WITH ICE

ICE
IS
MORE
DEPENDABLE

PURE, HEALTHFUL ICE

NO FOOD ODORS ABSORBED

Anderson Ice & Coal Co.
421 N. W. J St. (Plant)
22 N. 9th St. (Office)   Phone 1154

75

Permanent Drains—No Drip Pans to Empty

Requires Re-icing Every 4 to 7 Days Only

Plenty of Ice Cubes—No Expensive Repairs

THE KIMBALL COMPANY
ICE
NORTH THIRD ST.
PHONE 23-456
25 50 100 75

50
Form 42   4-49-15M FS
ICE SAVES FOOD
THE
UNION
ICE
COMPANY
PHONES
SAN PEDRO TERMINAL 3-3522
WILMINGTON TERMINAL 3-3408
LOMITA 426
GARDENA, MENLO 4-2024
Phone your first order; this display card
will be sufficient thereafter
100

40 lbs.
Nelson Ice Co.
ICE
30 lbs.   50 lbs.
15 Ekman Street
Tel. Dial 5-0746
60 lbs.

THIS SIDE UP INDICATES 15¢ PIECE
J. F. BELL & SONS CO.
ICE
THIS END UP 30¢ PIECE   THIS END UP 25¢ PIECE
THIS SIDE UP 20¢ PIECE
When No Ice Is Wanted Remove Card From Window
Smith & Town, Printers, Berlin, N. H.

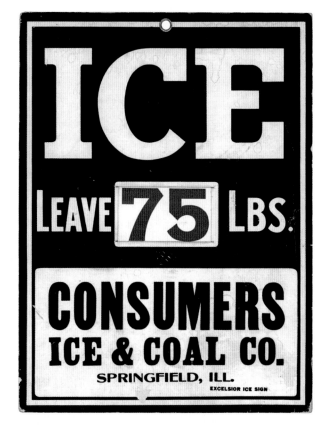

ICE
LEAVE 75 LBS.
CONSUMERS
ICE & COAL CO.
SPRINGFIELD, ILL.
EXCELSIOR ICE SIGN

IMPORTANT
This card is intended to aid us in giving our customers prompt service. Hang it in some conspicuous place where our driver can see it from the street. The Lower Corner when hanging indicates the amount of ice wanted.
Hang this Card Out Early.

Display With Amount Wanted on Top

Tebbits, Inc.
—
PHONE
22721

WELDON, WILLIAMS & LICK, FT. SMITH, ARK.

KRUGER BROS.
PURE
BIG STONE LAKE
ICE
PHONE 2571
HANG AMOUNT WANTED DOWN

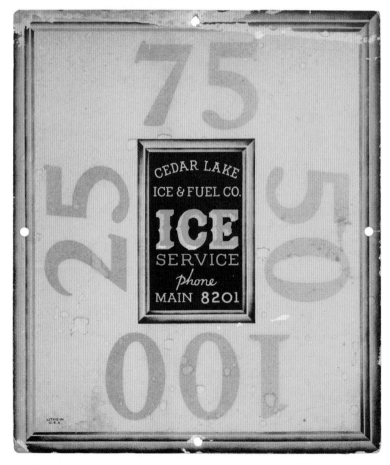

CEDAR LAKE
ICE & FUEL CO.
ICE
SERVICE
phone
MAIN 8201

LITHO IN U.S.A.

CENTRAL
CALIFORNIA
ICE CO.
—
Phone 2-6145

The Meridian Co., Inc., Union City, Ind.

50
TELEPHONE
ADAMS 1222
The Citizens Ice Company
(MEMBERS OF NATIONAL ASSOCIATION OF ICE INDUSTRIES)
**PLEDGED TO
PURITY~FULL WEIGHT~GOOD SERVICE**
25 75
100

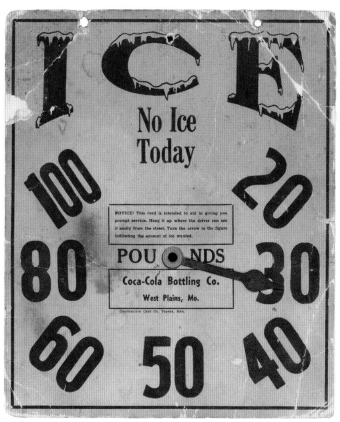

ICE
No Ice Today
100 20
NOTICE! This card is intended to aid in giving you prompt service. Hang it up where the driver can see it easily from the street. Turn the arrow to the figure indicating the amount of ice wanted.
POU●NDS
Coca-Cola Bottling Co.
West Plains, Mo.
Combination Card Co. Topeka, Kan.
80 30
60 50 40

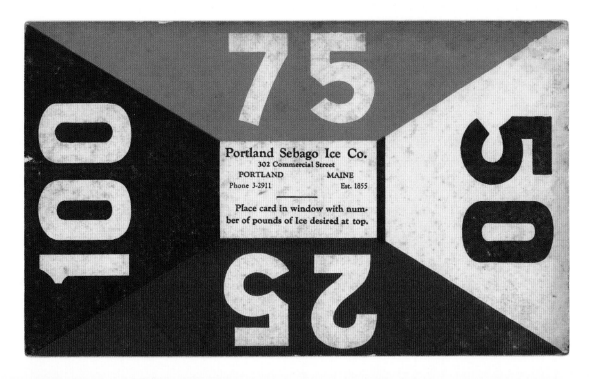

75
100
50
Portland Sebago Ice Co.
302 Commercial Street
PORTLAND   MAINE
Phone 3-2911   Est. 1855
Place card in window with number of pounds of Ice desired at top.
25

Icemen who cheated their customers inspired this cartoon and poem.

TO THE ICEMAN, BOSS OF CHEATS

Fierce, oh, fierce, would be our joy
To see you fixed like this, old boy,---
Frozen fast within a cake,
Out of which you could not break!

FAMILY ICE TONGS

FOR SALE HERE

Price_____

ASK TO SEE SAMPLE

VIVIAN HOUSEHOLD TONGS - VIVIAN MANUFACTURING CO., ST. LOUIS, MO., ICE TOOLS AND SUPPLIES

Families often owned ice tools such as tongs and ice picks or awls (used to break small pieces from an ice block).

Icemen were a vital part of people's lives. Some were honest and generous, but icemen, in general, were considered a necessary evil. When delivering ice, they often left puddles and muddy footprints on kitchen floors. Some also cheated. A New York City newspaper noted in 1890, "With ice selling at a cent a pound, it is easy for them to give short weight, and put a nickel or a dime in their pockets on almost every transaction during the day."

Every ice wagon had tools for cutting, tongs for carrying, and a scale for weighing ice. One New York customer noticed that his iceman "carelessly" left his heavy ice tongs on top of ice blocks as they were being weighed. A New York woman who paid for regular delivery of ice suspected the icemen of cheating. So she bought a scale. When an ice block came up to her apartment via a dumbwaiter (a small elevator used to raise and lower objects and packages), her scale showed that it had mysteriously lost as many as fifteen pounds in the half-minute trip up to her apartment! Once icemen knew she had her own scale, the cheating stopped.

ICE TONGS

Ice tongs were designed for different uses. Tongs with two handles linked together (Kansas City chain tongs, below) enabled a person to carry a block of ice with one hand. Market tongs (right-hand page) were used to hoist blocks high overhead (for example, into a ship). Platform delivery tongs (right-hand page) enabled men to lower an ice block a few feet without bending over.

NO. 540
BOSTON TONGS
Solid Handle.
Red. Points, ¾ in wide.

NO. 545
NEW YORK TONGS
Solid Handle.
Red. Narrow Points.

NO. 546½
MANHATTAN TONGS
Hollow Handle.
Red. Wide Points.

NO. 547
PHILADELPHIA TONGS
Solid Handle.
Black. Narrow Points.

NO. 550½
KANSAS CITY CHAIN TONGS
Black. Thin Points.

NO. 551
PATENT LINK TONGS
Black. Thin Points.

NO. 561
EASTERN EDGING-UP TONGS
Red. Narrow Points.
Weight, 4 lbs.

NO. 544
CAR TONGS
Hollow Handle.
Black. Points, ¾ in.wide.

NO. 555
BUFFALO TONGS
Chisel-shaped Points.
Weight, 2½ lbs.

NO. 578
MARKET TONGS

Single Point.
Red. Points, ¾ in. wide.
Weight, 8 lbs.

NO. 565
DRAG TONGS

Red. Points, ¾ in. wide.
Weight, 8 lbs.

NO. 579
MARKET TONGS

Double Point.
Red. Broad Points.
Weight, 8½ lbs.

NO. 569
PLATFORM DELIVERY
TONGS

Red. Narrow Points.
Weight, 4¼ lbs.

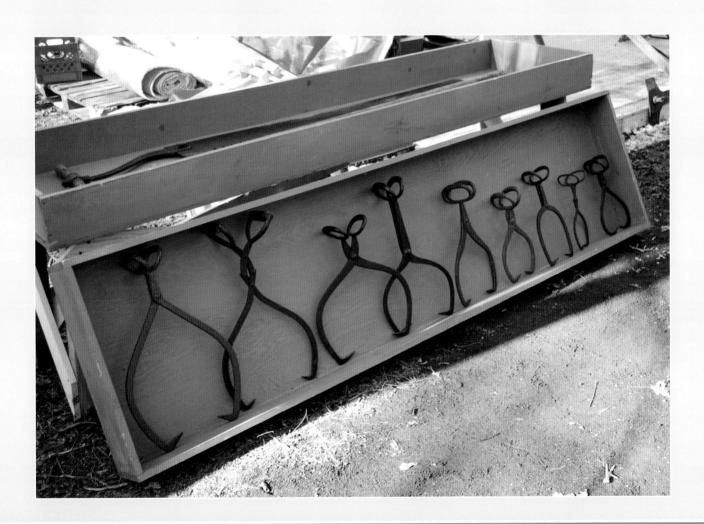

In the early 1900s, a cartoonist captured the excitement of children on a summer day, taking small pieces of ice from an ice delivery wagon.

Ice wagons hauled cooling loads through hot summer streets. Children came running when an ice wagon arrived. The iceman often cut ice blocks into smaller portions. Ice chips went flying. Some icemen offered the chips generously, but regardless, children usually tried to grab an icy treat. They often carried a cup or an empty tin can. A reporter described how children in Pittsburgh, Pennsylvania, used these containers: "They catch icy drippings beautifully; then when the iceman chops those huge blocks so many little pieces fly that a receptacle becomes absolutely necessary to the little treasure hunters."

ICE FAMINE!

In one way, the ice business was very much like farming. After several good years in a row, a farmer's crops might be ruined by a late frost or by a severe summer drought. Weather changes could also affect crops of ice. A January thaw could bring ice harvesting to a total halt. Ice companies and their workers were left to hope and wonder: would good ice weather return? Sometimes ice companies scrambled—reaching northward to colder climates, desperate to store enough ice to meet next summer's needs.

The first crisis of this kind struck in the winter of 1869–1870. Mild weather caused a poor harvest of ice from Rockland Lake, the Hudson River, and many other sources in Pennsylvania, Massachusetts, and other northeastern states. Ice companies in New York, Philadelphia, Baltimore, and Washington, D.C., paid high prices to have ice harvested and shipped from Maine.

Ice harvesting on the Kennebec River, with icehouses onshore, in Gardiner, Maine

People wait to pick up free ice in New York City in the early 1900s.

Ice Riot!

Sometimes poor families could not afford to keep an icebox chilled. Some cities set up distribution places that offered small amounts of ice for free. At six a.m. on July 20, 1906, five hundred people were lined up at such a site on the east side of Manhattan in New York City. They hoped to take home a four-pound piece of ice. However, the ice wagon was late, and some people had to be at work by seven a.m. The crowd grew anxious. The ice wagon arrived and icemen began to cut pieces to hand out.

One man left his place in line, pleading that he would be fined if he was late for work. This caused others to step out of line, and soon the ice wagon was surrounded by angry people. Then a woman pulled a man's mustache. Another woman hit a man with a dishpan. Men began punching one another. Soon hundreds were in a rough-and-tumble fight. A police officer ran to a telephone to call for help. When a patrol wagon loaded with police reserves arrived, they found no people—and no ice.

This led the Knickerbocker Ice Company and others to prepare for the next ice famine. It came a decade later. By then, major ice companies had bought land along Maine's Kennebec River. By February 1880, ice harvests to the south were failing, but ice on the Kennebec was up to eighteen inches thick. Ice-harvesting equipment was rushed to the Kennebec as well as to Maine's Penobscot and Sheepscot Rivers. Sawdust and salt hay, needed for insulation, suddenly became costly in Maine. That winter, a reporter estimated that on just four miles of the Kennebec River, an army of four thousand men and 350 horses worked day and night to harvest ice.

Ice famines were big trouble, because more and more people in the United States had come to rely on their iceboxes, which were supplied with regular deliveries of ice. Ordinary frozen water had become a kind of treasure. In the West, the discovery of gold sometimes sparked a mad scramble of men trying to make a fortune. That was called a "gold rush." In the East and Midwest, a mild winter sparked an "ice rush."

Ice was vital in everyone's life. Outside their school in Washington, D.C., children gather to watch an iceman lift an ice block with his tongs. (The ice had been shipped from faraway Maine.)

THE ICE INDUSTRY MELTS AWAY

The United States ice business reached its peak in the late 1800s. The national harvest of 1886 was estimated at more than twenty-five million tons. Icehouses numbering in the thousands were a dramatic symbol of this thriving business. In New York alone, between Rockland Lake and Albany, the state capital, at least 145 of these huge storage houses stood along the Hudson River in 1895.

The success of the ice business set the stage for its demise. An ice famine was headline news and a threat to a steady supply of ice. Once a luxury, refrigeration had become a necessity. People counted on having food and drink kept cold and safe. They would have continued to rely on iceboxes if something better hadn't come along.

Another kind of refrigeration was needed, and not just for reliability. Sewage and other wastes spoiled the quality of natural ice from lakes and rivers. To protect human health from pollution, ice harvesting was banned from some sites. The need grew for a safer kind of refrigeration. In the United States, the beer-brewing industry also spurred the development of artificial refrigeration. Lager beer could be brewed only at low temperatures.

For Some, No Nostalgia

One ice worker in New York State wrote: "Looking back I cannot see any romantic side to the ice harvest. It was just cold, hard work. . . . It is one industry that is not missed."

"PLENTY OF ICE FOR EVERYBODY."
—*New York Times*, September 13, 1881

"THE HUDSON RIVER ICE CROP.
A Full Harvest and No Fear of a Summer Famine."
—*New York Times*, February 13, 1886

"RUINING THE ICE CROP.
The Warm Rain Causes Much Damage on River and Ponds."
—*New York Times*, February 25, 1890

"NO ICE IN THE MAINE RIVERS."
—*New York Times*, January 10, 1892

"ICE HARVEST HALTED.
Warm Weather Brings Fear of Another Famine Next Summer."
—*New York Times*, January 5, 1907

As year-round beer sales increased, breweries didn't want to gamble on good ice harvests; they needed dependable refrigeration throughout every season.

Beginning in the 1840s, inventors registered dozens of patents for artificial-refrigeration machines. Most of these inventions failed. Eventually, an ice-making process that used compressed ammonia gas had some success. (The ammonia was recycled in the system.) These machines first supplied some ice for New Orleans and other Gulf Coast cities, where natural ice shipped from the faraway Northeast was very expensive. With time, the ammonia-compression process was improved. By the 1890s, all major breweries had giant ice-making machines. And by 1915, the same was true of all major meat-packing companies.

Iceboxes began to disappear in the early 1900s.

These commercial refrigerators were bulky and needed constant attention. They could not replace the common home icebox. However, iceboxes began to disappear in the early 1900s after successful demonstrations of a small electric-powered refrigerator (invented by a French physicist, Marcel Audiffren) that used sulfur dioxide as a coolant. From this beginning came modern refrigerators, powered by small electric motors. In the United States in 1926, companies sold two thousand of these refrigerators. Just eleven years later, in 1937, customers purchased three million.

The once mighty ice business slowly melted away. Thanks to the quality of Rockland Lake ice, its harvest continued longer than that of many less pure sources. The lake's last commercial ice was cut in 1924. Across the United States, however, many families and some businesses still needed ice for iceboxes until the 1950s, because not everyone was able to use an electric-powered refrigerator. It took decades for electrical lines to reach the entire country, especially rural America.

Refrigeration had become a necessity, and people depended on ice and iceboxes. Then electric-powered refrigerators (right) were invented. This photograph appeared in a 1930s advertisement.

Icehouses sometimes caught fire, as this one did in Southwick, Massachusetts. Wooden parts burned, but many tons of stored ice remained.

Hundreds of giant icehouses were abandoned. Their hulking white forms loomed like ghosts alongside lakes and rivers. Lacking windows, they were well suited for the business of growing mushrooms, and a few extended their usefulness in that role. Many were torn down, and some burned. In 1926, workers tearing down the last icehouse at Rockland Lake accidentally started a fire. A strong April wind drove the flames uphill, destroying many homes and other buildings in the village of Rockland Lake. For two more years, pockets of sawdust continued to smolder in the icehouse foundation.

At Rockland Lake, and near many other northern lakes and rivers, parts of stone foundations of icehouses still remain. Hidden in forests, overgrown by vines and other vegetation, they are silent reminders of an amazing time in American history. In some areas, at history museums and ice festivals, visitors can find displays of old photographs and old tools of the ice business. And some ice festivals celebrate the days when the winter ice of lakes and rivers bustled with working men and horses, and every home relied on its icebox and delivery by the iceman.

Hidden in a lakeside forest, a stone-and-concrete foundation is all that remains of a giant icehouse.

ICE SCULPTURES

Ice-sculpting and snow-sculpting contests are often part of many winter festivals held in northern states. At some of these events, the history of the ice business is celebrated. The ice sculptures shown here were photographed at the Knickerbocker Ice Festival, held at Rockland Lake, New York. They include a gargoyle (top right), Canada geese frozen in flight (bottom right), and an icy replica of the *Half Moon*, on which Henry Hudson explored the river now named for him in September 1609 (below).

Help in the Harvest

ICE
is needed to Save Food
for the Starving people
of the World

UNITED STATES
FOOD ADMINISTRATION

NATIONAL ASSOCIATION
OF ICE INDUSTRIES

World War I caused a call for help with the ice harvest. The United States did not enter the war until 1917. But before that, U.S. companies made weapons and ammunition for the country's European allies. Scarce supplies of ammonia were needed to make ammunition. The government ordered that ice-making machines (which used ammonia) be shut down during winter and early spring. This created a need for more natural ice and men to harvest and store it.

ACKNOWLEDGMENTS

I appreciate the assistance of the Historical Society of Rockland County, the Friends of Rockland Lake and Hook Mountain, and the library staff of the New-York Historical Society. Thanks to Florence Katzenstein for the temporary loan of the 1884 hand-tinted engraving *The Ice Industry of New York* (page 35) and to Brian Jennings, local-history librarian of the Nyack Library, for his assistance in tracking down old documents, photographs, and illustrations. I am especially grateful to the cofounders of the Knickerbocker Ice Festival: Rob Patalano, sculptor, Rockland Lake Ice Company; and Timothy Englert, filmmaker, artist, and, for four years, the development specialist for the Palisades Interstate Park Commission. They have educated many thousands of people—myself included—about the amazing history of the ice business. Also, many thanks to Gail and Thomas Lucia of Ice Box Memories for their generosity, expertise, and passionate interest in the icebox era. Finally, I am grateful for the work of my "teammates" at Calkins Creek and Boyds Mills Press, especially for the expertise and diligence applied to my writing by editor Carolyn P. Yoder and copy editor Joan Hyman, and for the colorful and appealing design of *ICE!* by Carla Weise and art director Barbara Grzeslo.

The cost of ice, delivered to homes, hotels, and restaurants, in 1901

1901 ICE 1901

CASH PRICES.

30 pounds,	10 cents.
50 pounds,	15 cents.
100 pounds,	20 cents.

100 to 300 pounds at one delivery,	20c per 100 lbs.
300 to 1000 pounds at one delivery,	15c " "
1000 pounds or more at one delivery,	12 1-2c " "

Shaved or chopped ice, 15c per basket.

BY SCORE.

Less than 50 pounds at one delivery,	30c per 100 lbs.
50 to 100 pounds at one delivery,	25c " "
100 to 300 pounds at one delivery,	20c " "
300 to 1000 pounds at one delivery,	15c " "
1000 pounds or more at one delivery,	12 1-2c " "

Shaved or chopped ice, 15c per basket.

All ice sold by weight.
No less than 10 cents' worth of ice carried into houses.
Ice at the ice-house same price as from wagons.
No ice delivered on Sunday.
All bills due the first day of each month.
Drivers are not allowed to change above prices or make contracts or rules other than these.
$1.00, $2.00, $5.00 and $10.00 coupon books for sale at the OFFICE at a discount of 10 per cent.
Customers will confer a favor by reporting to the office immediately any cause for complaint. Corrections cannot be made at the end of the season.

COCHICHEWICK LAKE ICE COMPANY.

Office: 430 Essex Street, Lawrence, Mass.

With F. P. Berry & Co.   Telephone 266-4.

FOR MORE INFORMATION

Website

Ice Box Memories

iceboxmemories.com

Visitors to this website can read about iceboxes, ice-harvesting tools, and the colorful cards that customers placed in their windows to tell icemen how much ice to deliver.

Museum

Knowlton's Ice Museum

317 Grand River Avenue, Port Huron, Michigan 48060

(810) 987-5441

bluewater.org/directory/knowltons-ice-museum

The website, which promotes tourism along the shores of eastern Michigan, offers access to this museum. The museum's site lists its hours of operation and visitor fees. Click on "Virtual Tour" to see panoramic views of exhibit rooms.

Ice-Harvesting Films*

Inventor Thomas Edison made short films, listed below, of ice harvesting at Rockland Lake, New York, in 1898 and 1902. They are preserved at the Library of Congress and can be viewed on YouTube.com. Enter the title of the film on YouTube's website, or use the web address provided below.

1898 Thomas Edison, Loading Ice on Cars by Thomas A. Edison, Inc.,
© February 24, 1902
youtube.com/watch?v=iQImPkUKJZo
See men loading ice onto railroad cars, two cars descending the steep slope to barges by the river, and ice being loaded onto a barge.

Circular Panorama of Housing the Ice by Thomas A. Edison, Inc.,
© February 24, 1902
youtube.com/watch?v=o5_jE0aCXkY&feature=relmfu
Watch blocks of ice carried up slanting elevators into an icehouse.

Cutting and Canaling Ice by Thomas A. Edison, Inc., © February 24, 1902
youtube.com/watch?v=Guqht4wtUX8
See men with horses pulling saws, marking the ice that will be cut into blocks. Catch a brief glimpse of a giant icehouse and the clove through which ice was transported to the Hudson River.

For Young Readers

The Ice Horse by Candace Christiansen. Paintings by Thomas Locker (Dial Books, 1993). This book of fiction (based on fact) is about ice harvesting on the Hudson River.

*Websites active at time of publication

SOURCE NOTES

The source of each quotation in this book is found below. The citation indicates the first words of the quotation and its document source. Almost all of the sources are listed in the bibliography. Complete citations are provided for those sources not in the bibliography.

page 3
"frozen water trade": Weightman, p. 12.
"Icebox of New York City": Cacioppo, p. 3B.

page 6
"gone already": George Washington, quoted in Jones,
    America's Icemen, p. 75.

page 8
"for transporting Ice . . .": quoted in Weightman, p. 21.
"People only laugh . . .": quoted in Crawford, p. 393.
"Ice King": Norton, p. 219.

"father of the ice industry": Bramen, Lisa. "The Ice King Cometh: Frederic Tudor, Father of the Ice Industry." *Food & Think* (blog), March 2, 2011. blogs.smithsonianmag.com/food/2011/03/the-ice-king-cometh-frederic-tudor-father-of-the-ice-industry/.*

"has never been . . .": quoted in Weightman, photo insert opposite p. 178.

page 9

"just enough of a schemer . . .": quoted in Weightman, p. 108.

"There is not a single tool . . .": *Boston Evening Transcript*, September 2, 1856, quoted in Weightman, p. 211.

page 15

"Ice has two . . .": *Godey's Lady's Book and Magazine*, p. 78.

page 17

"the pond": Dobbin, p. 1.

page 19

"for collecting, storing . . .": quoted in Stott, p. 9.

"increased the shipment . . .": Ibid.

page 23

"Sometimes nearly two hundred men . . .": John Burroughs, quoted in Lewis, p. 244.

"Ice or no ice . . .": Ibid.

page 25

"I would lead the horse . . .": Josephine Walter, quoted in Maroni, p. F1.

*Website active at time of publication

page 27

"silver harvest": *Merchants' Magazine and Commercial Review*, p. 177.

page 33

"The pure Walden water . . .": Henry David Thoreau, quoted in
  Weightman, p. 170.

page 45

"With ice selling at . . .": *Christian Union*, p. 42.

page 48

"They catch icy drippings . . .": *New York Times*, "Behind the Iceman's
  Back," p. 8.

page 51

"ice rush": Weightman, p. 228.

page 52

"Looking back I cannot see . . .": George W. Walter, quoted in Jones,
  America's Icemen, p. 20.

ICE AND THE MODERN Coolerator

The Air Conditioned Refrigerator

THE MOST HEALTHFUL AND ECONOMICAL REFRIGERATION

There is no need to place food in any certain place in the Coolerator, as the entire food compartment is always cold, whether the ice compartment is full or nearly empty.

Ice Only Every 4 to 7 Days

With the Coolerator most of the year the ice man will come only once a week, but even in the hottest climates it is never necessary to ice it oftener than every four days.

A good average for the year round is from four to six days.

This saving in ice alone will pay for the Coolerator.

Ice Cubes In 5 Minutes

Clear, sparkling ice cubes can be easily made if you have a Coolerator. By placing a Coolerator Automatic Ice Cuber on top of the ice block a good supply of crystal-clear ice cubes can be kept available at all times and at a very low cost.

1. Ice produces the correct cold temperature in a properly constructed refrigerator without sapping the moisture from the foods or drying them out.

2. Ice produces a constant air circulation which washes and purifies the air by carrying the odors and gases given off by the food to the surface of the ice, where

3. Melting ice produces the water which absorbs these gases and odors and carries them off through the drain pipe into the sewer.

Remember: For preserving natural foods, experience has demonstrated that ice is dependable, economical, and that it gives better results than any known form of refrigeration.

ASK YOUR ICE MAN

HE WILL BE GLAD TO TELL YOU MORE ABOUT ICE REFRIGERATION

IF IN NEED OF ICE PLEASE CALL OUR ORDER DEPARTMENT

DO NOT HESITATE TO CALL OUR ATTENTION TO ANY INEFFICIENCY IN THE SERVICE

MAIN 8201   **Cedar Lake Ice & Fuel Company**   **MAIN 8201**

CALL OUR FUEL DEPARTMENT FOR ● COAL COKE OIL OR WOOD

BIBLIOGRAPHY

BOOKS

Andreas, Alfred T. *History of Chicago.* Vol. 3. New York: Arno Press, 1884.

Crawford, Mary Caroline. *Old Boston Days & Ways: From the Dawn of the Revolution Until the Town Became a City.* Boston: Little, Brown, 1909.

Hill, Dewey D., and Elliott R. Hughes. *Ice Harvesting in Early America.* New Hartford, NY: New Hartford Historical Society, 1977.

Jackson, Donald, and Dorothy Twohig, eds. *The Diaries of George Washington.* Vol. 4. Charlottesville: University Press of Virginia, 1978.

Jones, Joseph C., Jr. *American Ice Boxes: A Book on the History, Collecting, and Restoration of Ice Boxes.* Humble, TX: Jobeco Books, 1981.

Jones, Joseph C., Jr. *America's Icemen: An Illustrative History of the United States Natural Ice Industry, 1665–1925.* Humble, TX: Jobeco Books, 1984.

During the first few decades of the 1900s, icebox makers advertised that their products were still better, and more "healthful," than electric-powered refrigerators. In the Coolerator, an ice block was placed in the upper compartment.

Lewis, Tom. *The Hudson: A History*. New Haven: Yale University Press, 1984.

Thoreau, Henry D. *Walden; or, Life in the Woods*. Boston: Ticknor and Fields, 1854.

Weightman, Gavin. *The Frozen-Water Trade: A True Story*. New York: Hyperion, 2003.

ARTICLES

Budke, George H. "Indians Had Their Reasons for Naming Nyack as They Did in Algonquian Tongue." *Journal News* (Nyack, NY), March 8, 1944, 1.

Cacioppo, Nancy. "Rockland Lake in Winter Became 'Icebox of New York City.'" *Journal News* (Nyack, NY), March 9, 2003, 3B.

Christian Union. "The Spectator." July 24, 1890, 42.

Cummings, H. T. "Ice; Its Collection, Storage and Distribution." *American Journal of Pharmacy*, May 1868, 211–224.

Dobbin, William J. "Rockland Lake." *South of the Mountain*, July–September 1963, 1–3.

Godey's Lady's Book and Magazine. "Ice Has Two Natural Enemies." July 1868, 78.

Krasner-Khait, Barbara. "The Impact of Refrigeration." *History Magazine*, February–March 2003, 41–44.

Maine Farmer. "The Ice Fields." January 10, 1895, 4.

Maroni, Peter. "Growing Up at Rockland Lake." *Journal News* (Nyack, NY), May 19, 1985, F1–F2.

Merchants' Magazine and Commercial Review. "Ice: And the Ice Trade." August 1, 1856, 169–180.

New York Times. "Behind the Iceman's Back." September 7, 1906, 8.

New York Times. "Horse Lived Two Lives." July 20, 1909, 7.

New York Times. "May Give Free Ice to the City's Poor." June 10, 1919, 28.

New York Times. "Police Reserves Needed to Quell Ice Riot." July 20, 1906, 14.

Norton, Charles Ledyard. "The Midwinter Harvest." *Chautauquan: A Weekly Newsmagazine,* January 1887, 219–222.

Providence Journal (in *Current Literature,* 1888–1912). "Ice Cutting in New England: An American Winter Industry." March 1897, 269–272.

Scientific American. "The Ammonia Ice-Making Process." April 18, 1874, 243.

Scientific American. "Improved Corpse Preserver." December 6, 1862, 360.

Stott, Peter. "The Knickerbocker Ice Company and Inclined Railway at Rockland Lake." *Journal of the Society for Industrial Archeology* 5, no. 1 (1979): 7–18.

Youth's Companion. "Whose Tongs Were They?" November 25, 1897, 598.

IMAGE CREDITS

American Agriculturist, 1869: 20, 27 (bottom).

Myles Aronowitz/Lush Photography: 58, 59 (bottom).

Charles E. Frohman Collection, Hayes Presidential Center: 9.

Timothy J. Englert: 59 (top).

Gifford-Wood Co., *Ice Harvesting Machinery and Tools*, reprinted from General Catalog No. 18, 1919: 10, 27 (top), 28–29.

Gleason's Drawing Room Companion, 1852: 22.

The Granger Collection, New York: left of title page; 11, 12, 26, 55.

Harper's Weekly, August 30, 1884, loaned by Florence Katzenstein: 35.

Ice Box Memories, Thom and Gail Hogan Lucia, Springfield, Massachusetts: front and back jacket, spine, back flap, half-title page, 1, 2, 14, 39, 40–41, 42–43, 44, 45, 49, 51, 56, 62, 68.

Library of Congress, Prints and Photographs Division: LC-USZ62-114925: 4; FSA/OWI Collection, LC-USW3-022756-C: 6 (inset); Detroit Publishing Company Collection, LC-D401-13653: 50; Prints and Photographs Division: LC-USZC4-3186: 60.

Collection of The New-York Historical Society: 21.

Nyack Library Local History Collection: 18, 25, 30, 31, 32, 33, 34.

Old Boston Days & Ways, by Mary Caroline Crawford, 1909: 8.

Courtesy of Palisades Interstate Park Commission archives: 24.

Laurence Pringle: 6 (top), 19, 47 (bottom), 57.

Scientific American, December 6, 1862: 13; March 27, 1875: 36.

American Illustrators Robert Fawcett Stamp © 2001 **United States Postal Service.** All Rights Reserved. Used with Permission: 7.

Wikimedia Commons: 16.

Wisconsin Historical Society, WHi-89604: 48.

Wm. T. Wood & Co. *Ice Tools Catalog*, 1885: 46, 47 (top).

INDEX

Page numbers in **boldface** refer to photographs and/or captions.